KINGFISHER KNOWLEDGE

SPIES

SPIES

Clive Gifford

Foreword by
Dame Stella Rimington

KINGFISHER

GO FURTHER...

INFORMATION PANEL KEY:

websites and
further reading

career paths

places to visit

KINGFISHER

Kingfisher Publications Plc
New Penderel House,
283–288 High Holborn,
London WC1V 7HZ
www.kingfisherpub.com

Publishing manager: Melissa Fairley
Senior designer: Carol Ann Davis
Picture research manager: Cee Weston-Baker
DTP manager: Nicky Studdart
Production controller: Lindsey Scott
Artwork archivists: Wendy Allison, Jenny Lord
Proofreader: Sheila Clewley
Indexer: Diana Le Core

First published by Kingfisher Publications Plc 2004
First published in paperback 2007

10 9 8 7 6 5 4 3 2 1
1TR/1206/TWP/MA(MA)/130ENSOMA/F

ISBN 978 0 7534 1065 3

Copyright © Kingfisher Publications Plc 2004

Contents

Foreword

Every country has secret services to help protect it against serious threats from terrorists, major criminals or even from other countries. People who threaten to harm a country always plot in secret, so the intelligence agencies have to work in secret to find out what is being planned before it happens, so that it can be prevented. They do that in many different ways – by secretly listening to their targets talking on the phone, by planting microphones to overhear meetings, by watching the targets as they move from place to place and by recruiting some of the targets to act as double agents to report on what is going on. The information that comes from all these sources is called 'intelligence' and the organizations that gather it are called intelligence services.

For most of my career I worked in one of the UK's three intelligence services, MI5, the domestic security service. I first joined in the 1970s, in the middle of the Cold War, when the world was divided into two armed camps, the Soviet Union and its allies on the one side and Western Europe, America and their allies on the other. The Cold War never became a fighting war. It was an intelligence war, with intelligence officers from both sides trying to find out what the other side was doing, what kind of weapons they had, when and if they might start a war and what their plans were. Both sides were secretly working in each other's countries. One of my jobs in MI5 was to try to find out who the Soviet intelligence officers in the UK were and what they were up to; to try to stop them finding out any of the UK's secrets and to recruit them to our side to act as double agents. We followed them, listened to their telephone conversations and got to know our targets, so we could suggest they spy for us as double agents. If they refused we made them leave the country and go home, where they could not do so much harm.

Nowadays one of the biggest threats to the world comes from terrorists. Intelligence officers from many different countries are working together to find out who they are, where they are and what they are planning. Today's MI5 officers get their intelligence in much the same way as we did during the Cold War, but their task is even more difficult and urgent because most terrorists want to kill people. Many terrorist attacks that are planned and prepared never happen, and we never know anything about them because the intelligence services find out about the planned attacks and prevent them. But they can never find out everything, however hard they work, so, sadly, a small number of terrorist attacks are successful. If a terrorist attack occurs, the intelligence agencies efforts turn to finding out who carried out the attack and getting them arrested.

Being an intelligence officer is vital and often exciting work, and it will always be needed. Even if terrorism stops, another threat will take its place. Whatever that threat is, secret intelligence work will be very important in tackling it.

Stella Rimington

Dame Stella Rimington, former Director-General of MI5

CHAPTER 1

Why spy?

When people think of spies, they imagine a dangerous but glamorous modern world of fast cars, elaborate gadgets and secret weapons. Yet spying is an ancient art and profession with a history stretching back thousands of years. In fact, ever since there have been secrets, there have been spies seeking out those secrets. Spying is all about obtaining information others do not wish to share. For companies, governments, military forces and even individuals, information equals power. This power, to know what an enemy or rival is thinking, planning or building, can be crucial – whole governments and countries may flourish or perish as a result.

Why do nations spy?

Spying is about getting an advantage over a rival or enemy while making sure your own secrets stay secure. Every nation spies. Even nations that appear friendly, and whose leaders meet regularly, usually conduct spying operations behind each other's backs. The rewards, in the form of intelligence (information), are simply too great, important and tempting not to do so.

National security

Every government has a duty to protect its country and people. The most common way to do this has been through building up large military forces while trying to gain intelligence through spying on the forces of other countries. Spies can find out what weapons another country has, where they are located, and what plans there may be for their use.

For over 40 years after World War II (1939–1945), many countries of the world aligned themselves with one of the two superpowers, the USA or the Soviet Union (now divided into 14 countries, including Russia). This period was known as the Cold War (1945–1991). The two giant nations were highly suspicious of each other and built up huge spying networks to monitor their rival's military actions.

▶ This aerial photograph, taken by an American spyplane in 1962, shows a missile base under construction on the island of Cuba. Previously, the Soviet Union's missiles had lain thousands of kilometres away from major US cities, but now they were located just 230km from the US state of Florida. The US government went public with this information and a period of heightened tension, known as the Cuban Missile Crisis, occurred before the missiles were withdrawn.

Stealing science secrets

As science has advanced, so too has the desire to learn how far ahead rivals are in developing new weapons. The race to make the first atomic bomb, for example, produced a period of spying throughout World War II and into the Cold War. The US atomic programme was ultra-top secret and a number of spies were caught passing on information to the Soviets. Yet other agents were not detected and in 1949, just a few years after America's first atomic test, the Soviet Union tested its first atomic weapon.

Know your enemy

As spying has grown in scale, and become more sophisticated, greater efforts are made to spy on other nations' spy networks. The sum of this work is to find out how other nations' spies operate, what information they are after and how their network can be infiltrated. It is also performed to find breaches in a country's own intelligence organizations.

Sometimes spies manage to operate in secret inside an opposing organization for long periods. Larry Wu Tai Chin (1923–1986), an operative in the CIA, for example, passed secrets to China for 30 years before he was caught.

These trailers hold oxidizer, a substance used to provide a missile's rocket with a supply of oxygen with which to burn its fuel.

FUEL TRAILERS

OXIDIZER TRAILERS

OXIDIZER TRAILERS

Early spies

▲ The King of Macedonia and one of the world's greatest military leaders, Alexander the Great used spies to discover the location and numbers of enemy armies.

No one knows the name of the world's first spy. But we do know that spies and scouts have been at work for thousands of years. Ever since people felt threatened by a rival group or tribe, scouts and spies were used to find out when and how an enemy might attack. There are dozens of references to spies and spying in the Bible; for instance, Moses sent 12 agents to report on the strength of the forces in the land of Canaan. Ancient civilizations, including the ancient Egyptians, Greeks and Romans, all used spies to build and maintain their empires.

The art of war

Between 500 and 400BCE, a Chinese diplomat and military strategist called Sun Tzu wrote *The Art of War* in which he advocated spying as a vital way to overcome an enemy. Sun Tzu believed that 'an army without secret agents is exactly like a man without eyes or ears'. In his book, he described different types of spies, and explained how techniques such as blackmail could be used to convert enemy spies.

▶ From the 8th to 9th century CE onwards, for almost 1,000 years, powerful feuding Japanese families employed Ninja warriors (right) as spies to infiltrate a rival's close circle of advisors. The Ninja were so adept at disguise that many people believed they had the power of invisibility.

To spy and conquer

In the distant past, great military commanders, such as Julius Caesar (100–44BCE) and Alexander the Great (356–323BCE), all used spies and spying techniques in order to conquer great areas of land for their empires. Roman emperor Julius Caesar, fearful of his instructions to generals and close advisors being intercepted, coded his messages by shifting each letter of the alphabet three places forward. This codewriting technique is known today as the Caesar Alphabet.

Mongol warlord Ghengis Khan (c.CE1162–1227) made great use of spies in the 13th century as he built an enormous empire that stretched from China in the east to parts of Europe in the west. As he expanded his territory outside Mongolia, Khan realized that the distinctive facial features of the Mongol peoples would quickly be spotted in foreign lands. So he recruited spies from local peoples to collect information on an enemy's forces.

◀ Sir Francis Walsingham (c.1530–1590), shown to the right of Queen Elizabeth I (1533–1603), uncovered the Babington Plot of 1586. Anthony Babington (1561–1586) was plotting to kill the queen and used a messenger called Gilbert Gifford (1561–1590) to smuggle secret messages to and from Mary Queen of Scots (1542–1587). What Babington did not know was that Gifford was a double agent, a spy who is used against his original master, under the control of Walsingham. Using a code-breaking expert, Walsingham trapped Babington and he, the other conspirators and Mary Queen of Scots were all executed.

Spies in Europe

Spying developed greatly in the 15th, 16th and 17th centuries CE as the struggle for supremacy between the European countries intensified. In the 15th century, a number of city-states formed embassies in, and sent ambassadors to, the major cities of Europe to gather information.

In France, the first major spy network was organized by Cardinal Richelieu (1585–1642), a powerful leader of the Catholic Church. In 1620, he set up a network of advisors called the Cabinet Noir to analyze reports, information and letters captured from his enemies by his own spies.

L'ESPIONNAGE

▲ This 1914 magazine cover publicizes the great fear of enemy spies held by many people at the outbreak of World War I (1914–1918). Campaigns in Britain in World War II warned people of enemy spies in their midst.

Spies at war (part one)

Though they are important in peacetime, spies become vital during war. Wartime spies can be a powerful weapon, discovering in advance where and when the enemy is planning to attack, how it plans to move and what kinds of weapons it is using. For many centuries, spies have also been employed to spread incorrect facts, called disinformation, to confuse an enemy's leaders or to spread rumours and panic amongst its people. Ghengis Khan (see page 10) and his Mongol armies, for example, used spies sent into enemy towns and fortresses to confuse, demoralize and divide an opposing force. Spies are also sent into enemy-held territory to help forces hostile to the enemy, known as resistance movements.

◄ Decorated for bravery during World War I, Josip Broz Tito (1892–1980) worked undercover in the 1920s and 1930s, organizing underground Communist Party groups in his native Yugoslavia (now Serbia). During World War II, Tito, shown in the centre planning a campaign with his aides, defeated German forces.

The secret of success

Many successful generals, such as Britain's Duke of Wellington (1769–1852) and the first American President, George Washington (1732–1799), built spy rings and networks to inform their forces and to stay one step ahead of the enemy. During America's Revolutionary War (1775–1783), President George Washington maintained the Culper Ring, a spy network in New York (home to the enemy British forces), which successfully warned Washington of attacks. Washington also employed double agents to misinform the British of his plans, tricking them into moving their armies away from targets he intended to attack. Intelligence passed on by spies in December 1776 allowed Washington's forces to cross the Delaware river and capture the important garrison of Trenton.

▶ Four intelligence officers working for the Union Army of the Potomac, USA, pose for a photograph during the American Civil War. By the end of the war, the Union intelligence operation controlled a large network of scouts and spies.

▲ Belle Boyd (1843–1900) spied for the Confederate forces during the American Civil War. Operating from her father's hotel in Front Royal, in the US state of Virginia, Boyd mingled with the Union soldiers occupying her town, collecting military secrets and ferrying documents across enemy lines.

▶ Dutch-born Margaretha Zelle, better known by her stage name Mata Hari, was famous throughout Europe as an exotic dancer before World War I. She supplied confidential information to both French and German authorities before she was betrayed and executed.

A risky business

Spying is always a risky business, but in wartime, capture can frequently mean torture and death, especially if a military spy dresses as a civilian.

During the American Revolutionary War, a British spy, Major John Andre (1750–1780), was caught and hanged by the Americans. The same fate befell an American for the first time when Nathan Hale (1755–1776), disguised as a Dutch schoolteacher, was caught spying on British forces in New York. His coded notes were found hidden in his shoe.

Women at war

During a number of conflicts, such as the American Civil War (1861–1865) and the world wars, spymasters found that where an adult male might arouse suspicion in an occupied region, women were usually allowed to pass and continue their travels or work.

For that reason, many women worked as spies for both the Union and Confederate sides during the American Civil War, including a former black slave, Mary Elizabeth Bowser (c.1839–unknown). Posing as an illiterate servant, she served dinner at the home of the Confederate president, Jefferson Davis (1808–1889), and was ignored as she stood listening in on military plans, before reporting back to Union forces. Some female spies, such as Mata Hari (1876–1917), became close friends or lovers with generals or politicians to obtain vital secrets.

Spies at war (part two)

Spying during both world wars reached new levels of organization, complexity and scale as hundreds of spies, from the dozens of nations caught up in the conflicts, sought out secrets. Some of the techniques they used, such as observation and disguise, had ancient origins, while others were brand new, such as complex cipher machines, coded messages broadcast over public radio services, and parachuting into enemy territory. Many of today's major secret services developed from these wartime operations.

▲ World War II double agent, Dusan Popov (above), met author Ian Fleming (1908–1964) in 1941 and proved to be the inspiration for Fleming's spy character, James Bond.

▲ Spies used a range of devices which could be hidden or disguised easily. This map of a part of France is printed on a small silk scarf.

▼ Odette Sansom revisits the French café in Arles where, during World War II, she would wait anxiously for messages from Britain to her resistance group.

Intercepting information

Information obtained during wartime can sometimes mean the difference between victory and defeat. In January 1917, for instance, British code-breakers intercepted and deciphered a telegram sent by the German Foreign Minister. It revealed how Germany planned to offer an alliance with Mexico in order to provoke a war with the USA, which had yet to enter World War I. Public outrage at the telegram played a major part in the USA declaring war on Germany.

Working with the resistance

During World War II, Britain's SOE was formed to work with resistance movements hostile to the occupying German forces. SOE agents such as Odette Sansom (1912–1995) were sent into occupied territory where they would help train resistance workers, be part of the process of gathering information on German forces, lead sabotage missions (see page 16) and act as couriers. Sansom was captured and tortured by the German Gestapo but refused to betray colleagues and survived the war.

▶ These British soldiers are on a World War II training exercise that involves a 'German spy', disguised as a woman, on the attack.

Spies in the Pacific

Japanese spy Takeo Yoshikawa (1916–unknown) posed as a tourist on the Hawaiian island of Oahu, and was able to observe ship and plane movements in and out of the major US naval base of Pearl Harbor.

Yugoslav-born Dusan 'Dusko' Popov (1912–1981) was one of several spies who alerted the Americans to Japanese activity in the Pacific, but this information was not acted upon.

◄ Fearing a Japanese invasion, Russia set up a spy ring in Japan, headed by Richard Sorge (1895–1944). After learning that Japan did not intend to attack, the Russians moved thousands of troops to the war on their western front against Germany. Sorge was executed by the Japanese. Here, his chief prosecutor (left) appears at a US investigation.

Sabotage and assassination

Spying is a deadly game and some missions, such as assassinations or sabotage operations, are designed to be especially destructive. Occasionally, a spy is forced to kill during action to successfully complete a mission. An assassination mission is different, however, as the kill is the entire focus – to remove a person considered a threat to national security. Sabotage missions seek to destroy part of a nation or group's infrastructure – its buildings, facilities, industry, transport or communications links.

Prime targets

Sabotage and assassination missions are vital wartime operations, but they also occur in peacetime. Saboteurs can help cripple industry or, by attacking a research centre, delay its scientific progress. A series of sabotage attempts can be carried out to disrupt another country's economy in the hope that this will lead to civil unrest and regime change (the overthrow of the existing government). To this end, secret services sometimes train rebel groups in other countries in the arts of sabotage.

Sabotage missions can also target the equipment or buildings of pressure groups. In 1985, *Rainbow Warrior*, the ship of environmental group Greenpeace, was moored in New Zealand prior to heading into the Pacific Ocean to try to disrupt and protest at French nuclear testing in the region. Two French secret service agents laid mines, sinking the *Rainbow Warrior* and killing one man.

▶ An intended assassination victim is caught in the crosshairs of a rifle's telescopic sight as the assassin homes in on his target. Security services do not just plan and carry out assassinations, they also work hard to protect their country's leaders from the threat of assassination.

◀ An agent lays explosives on railway tracks in order to derail a train. During World War II, saboteurs used bombs and mines to destroy bridges, railway lines, fuel dumps and airfields in occupied Europe to slow the movements of German troops.

► This Hi-Standard Model B.22 calibre pistol was modified by technical officers in the American OSS during World War II so that it could be reloaded and operated as quietly as possible. The silencer, fitted to the gun's barrel, reduced the noise from a shot.

Caught in the crosshairs

There have been many assassination attempts on leaders of countries. Some, such as the French SDECE's attempts on the life of Egypt's President Nasser during the 1950s, and more recent attempts on Saddam Hussein (1937–), have been unsuccessful. Dissidents, critics of a country's government, are key targets for assassins, as are spies who give up their trade or switch sides. In 1954, Nikolai Khokhlov (1922–), a KGB assassin, defected to West Germany. Three years later, the KGB poisoned him, but medical care enabled him to survive.

Deadly weapons

Assassins use a range of different weapons and techniques and, in most cases, must work stealthily so that their actions cannot be traced back to their security service. In the 1950s, KGB assassin Bogdan Stashinsky (1931–) used a spray gun, which fired a poisonous cyanide gas, to kill Lev Rebet (unknown–1957), a critic of the Soviet regime. The poison triggered a heart attack in its victims, giving the appearance of natural death, not murder.

▼ An armed guard lies in wait, equipped with a rifle fitted with a telescopic sight. Snipers, armed with high-powered, long-range rifles can pick off a target more than 1km away.

Industrial espionage

Industrial espionage involves spying on companies or organizations to learn what innovations and plans they have for their business, and illegally gaining the secrets of a new product's design, technology, formula or manufacturing process. Researching and developing a new product can take many years and cost millions of pounds. For some companies, uncovering a rival's product is a quicker and more cost-effective way of gaining an advantage. Industrial espionage is also performed by nations spying on another nation's businesses.

Stealing commercial secrets

All large companies keep a close watch on their rivals by monitoring the media and using close contacts to determine what they plan next. But some go further and actively 'steal' a rival's secrets by employing security specialists to infiltrate another company's offices, to hack into their computers or to rummage through their dustbins, in order to obtain vital documents. These companies may also choose to bribe an employee from a rival company.

A long history

Industrial espionage is not a new phenomenon. Around CE533, the secret of how to make silk was smuggled out of China.

At the start of the 19th century CE, Britain led the world in textiles manufacturing benefiting from the stolen Chinese invention. In 1810 and 1811, American Francis Cabot Lowell (1775–1817) visited England and Scotland and studied the machinery used in Britain's textile mills. Committing the details of the machinery to memory, Lowell was able to 'steal' the technology and build his own mill in the USA.

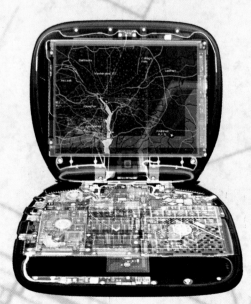

◄ Armed with little more than a laptop computer and the correct passwords, an industrial spy may be able to access a company's confidential files over a computer network unless it is carefully protected.

Bugs can be fitted in ceiling panels to pick up conversations at high-level meetings.

Stairwells are often meeting points for off-the-record conversations.

Pot plants provide space and cover to place microphones to transmit conversations.

▼ Many companies are becoming increasingly vigilant about the security of their secrets, employing guards, electronic locks, ID cards for their employees and making their computer systems more secure. Yet in lots of busy offices, there remain many potential ways for spies to seek out important, confidential information.

Tiny cameras can be fitted behind a clock to record video and sound.

A trusted employee may in fact be a double agent for another company, paid to collect sensitive information by talking to colleagues or collecting documents.

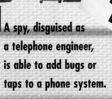

A spy, disguised as a telephone engineer, is able to add bugs or taps to a phone system.

Supersonic spying

During the 1960s, the race was on to develop the first airliner capable of flying faster than the speed of sound. The undoubted front-runner was the Anglo-French Concorde design, but the Soviet Union caused a sensation at the 1965 Paris Airshow when it unveiled its prototype airliner, the TU-144, which bore an incredible resemblance to Concorde. A Soviet spy, Sergei Fabiew, had supplied the Soviet Union with a complete set of Concorde blueprints. The TU-144 first flew at the end of 1968, beating Concorde's maiden flight by months.

High-tech secrets

Many military and government projects often have value in the commercial world. Industrial spies working for companies or governments find out secrets from these projects, and sell them to the highest bidder. In 1992, an American scientist, Dr Ronald Hoffman, was caught, having received £500,000 in payments from a range of Japanese clients for top secret computer programs he had sold to them. The programs had been developed for the SDI, better known as the Star Wars missile defence system.

◄ Details of a company's new computer chip can be worth millions to a rival which will pay a high price for a copy of the blueprints.

Spying on the public

Modern secret services do not just spy on rival nations, they also spy on their own citizens by working with police and other security services, and using camera, sensor and computer technology. For some people, the prospect of being spied upon is chilling and a severe invasion of privacy. Others feel that if this spying catches terrorists and major criminals, and combats the rising levels of serious crimes, such as drug-trafficking, then the cost to an individual's personal freedom is worthwhile.

Eyes everywhere

Security cameras taking individual still images or video footage have been placed in banks, shops, factories and offices for many years. Yet in the past decade, there has been an explosion in the number of CCTV (Closed Circuit Television) cameras placed in public locations, such as city centres, shopping malls, outside schools and along roads and motorways. According to the Sheffield Centre for Criminological Research, there are over four million CCTV cameras monitoring the public in Britain.

Other nations have also invested in large numbers of cameras, most of which are controlled by police forces or security companies. CCTV images are vital evidence for solving crimes, as they often capture criminals in the act. Images from many CCTV cameras are time- and date-stamped, enabling police to place a suspect or witness at a particular location at a precise time.

▶ Three CCTV cameras sit perched on a pole looking down on a city street. Footage from such cameras is sometimes used by secret services to identify movements of spies and suspects.

▼ A policeman sitting in a police surveillance room in Monaco scans a bank of monitors displaying real-time images from a battery of 60 cameras — and Monaco is only 2 km² in size.

▶ Monitors linked to a security camera system provide a security force with extra sets of eyes, especially valuable at major international events. At the 2000 Sydney Olympics, for example, extensive CCTV systems complemented the 4,000 security personnel from military forces and the ASIO.

Tracing and tracking

CCTV cameras are not the only way in which the public can be spied upon. Electronic tolls on roads in France, Germany and other European nations, along with traffic radar systems and electronic systems which can read vehicles' licence plates, can be used to monitor journeys. Computer records of a person's transactions with their credit cards can be accessed to trace their movements, while computer-based communications such as emails can also be tracked (see page 56). When tracing a potential criminal suspect, police may use spying techniques, including surveillance (see pages 38–39).

Working together

Many nations' secret services work closely with their country's law enforcement forces and international crime-fighting organizations such as Interpol. The US secret services, for example, have two main purposes: to protect US leaders, their families and visiting dignitaries, and to fight lawlessness. By sharing intelligence, the secret services and the police are able to help each other fight serious crimes such as the planting of bombs by terrorists, or drug-trafficking.

▲ An image from a security camera shows a pedestrian walking across the street in the town of Levallois Perret, just north of Paris, France. In 1994, this was the first place in France where security cameras observed public spaces. Today, hundreds of thousands of CCTV cameras can be found in France.

SUMMARY OF CHAPTER 1: WHY SPY?

Why is spying important?
Spies can obtain important information about rival countries, their future intentions and their military and economic ability. They can also discover another nation's scientific or technological secrets, as well as uncover plots and conspiracies that threaten a country's government.

When does spying occur?
Spies have been used for many thousands of years all over the world. They work both in peacetime and during wars. Many spies work for government and military secret services. But a few work alone or for rebel groups.

Is spying just about obtaining information?
Not always – a spy's mission can be to help destabilize a government, to damage or destroy a building, or sabotage a computer network of a rival intelligence service. On rare occasions, spies are ordered to carry out an assassination mission to kill someone threatening national security.

Do spies target businesses and the public?
Yes, spies work on obtaining a country's or company's commercial secrets for profit. Spying on the public does occur, especially as part of efforts to tackle major crime.

A Leica spy camera complete with lenses and filters

Go further...

 Read more about one of the world's most famous female spies, Mata Hari: www.crimelibrary.com/spies/mata_hari/

Learn about the lives of ten notorious 20th-century CE spies: www.pbs.org/wgbh/nova/venona/

Read answers from US Secret Service staff to children's questions about life working to protect others: www.secretservice.gov/kids_faq.shtml

True World War II Stories by Clive Gifford (Hodder Children's Books, 2002)

Undercover Agents by Paul Thomas (Belitha Press, 1997)

 Network security specialist
Protects companies' and security services' computer networks from attack by hackers and opposing security services.

Aerial reconnaissance officer
Organizes and analyzes images taken from satellites and aircraft to provide intelligence briefs.

Linguist
Translates and interprets information collected from telephone, post, internet and other forms of communication and analyzes messages for important data.

CCTV technician
Installs, maintains and upgrades CCTV cameras and systems.

 Take a trip to the Herefordshire museum dedicated to one intrepid World War II spy called Violette Szabo (1921–1945).
Violette Szabo Museum
Cartref
Wormelow
Hereford
England
HR2 8HN
Telephone: +44 (0) 1981 540477
www.violette-szabo-museum.co.uk

Check out the wartime spying exhibits at the Imperial War Museum, London.
Imperial War Museum
Lambeth Road
London SE1 6HZ
Telephone: +44 (0) 20 7416 5320
www.iwm.org.uk

CHAPTER 2

Spies and secret services

There are many different kinds of spy, each with a great variety of skills and attributes. Some spies are experts in gaining a potential contact's confidence, others are technical specialists in communications, languages, code-breaking, or they are skilled at breaking into a building or fitting bugs or phone taps. Some agents are expert saboteurs or trained killers, others analyze top secret data collected by other spies in the field. Whatever their skills and roles, most of the world's spies work for intelligence-gathering organizations known as secret services. Almost all the nations of the world have at least one secret service agency.

Secret services

France has the DGSE, Germany has the BND, and in Russia there is the SVR. The USA has the CIA, NSA and FBI, while Britain has MI5 and MI6. These abbreviations stand for some of the world's best-known secret services (see full list of names on page 61). While the names and some of the work that these organizations perform are known, much of their operation remains shrouded in mystery. Secret services are relatively young organizations. Nearly all began in the 20th century CE, but it did not take long for some to build a fearsome reputation.

Sharing duties

In many countries, organizations exist that spy within the home country or abroad. Britain's MI6 is one of the oldest secret services still in existence. It collects foreign intelligence, and was formed in 1909, the same year as its counterpart, MI5, which deals with security threats inside the country. MI5 was founded to identify and counter German spies then working in Britain.

Large countries, such as Russia and the USA, have many intelligence agencies. In the USA, spying abroad is conducted by the CIA, while the NSA is responsible for the security of communications and cryptology (code-making and code-breaking). America's FBI is a crime-fighting force, but it works mainly within the USA's borders.

Mossad

Israel's most important secret service is Mossad. Formed in 1951, it is active in, and maintains secret agents in, many countries around the world, particularly its Arab neighbours in the Middle East. Mossad agents have taken part in a number of high-profile missions, including the 1960 kidnapping of a former Nazi, Adolf Eichmann (1906–1962), from Argentina back to Israel where he stood trial for war crimes. Mossad agents also stormed a hijacked airliner in Uganda in 1976, rescuing 93 of the 97 hostages. One of Mossad's most celebrated spies was Elie Cohen (1924–1965) who, in the 1960s, infiltrated the top levels of the government of Syria.

◀ The official insignia (badge) of the KGB. The KGB spied inside and outside the Soviet Union. Russia's chief foreign intelligence agency is now the SVR.

▼ The Pentagon, home to the US Department of Defense, the world's biggest defence department, is also the world's largest office.

◀ The most famous employee of Britain's MI6 is the fictional spy James Bond, who was created by author Ian Fleming in 1952.

The eye-catching headquarters of MI6 (insignia above) stand on the banks of the River Thames in London, England. Fitted with bomb- and bullet-proof walls and triple-glazed windows which prevent electronic eavesdropping, the building's most sensitive areas are located deep underground.

Using more than 175,000 informers, it carried records on five million of its own people, around a third of the population. The Stasi often collaborated with the KGB, the Soviet Union's premier secret service. The KGB relied heavily on agents and informers to gain intelligence from around the world, and had many notable successes, including stealing US atomic secrets and the Cambridge spy ring (see page 30). Some of its recruits, including Robert Hanssen (see page 33) were only caught after the KGB had been disbanded in 1991 and its successor, the SVR, was in place.

The Stasi and KGB

One of the most feared of all secret services was the East German Stasi, created in 1950 and only disbanded with the reunification of Germany in 1989. The Stasi and East Germany's secret police, including the foreign intelligence section called the HVA, employed over 80,000 full-time officers.

▶ A training instructor for the CIA (insignia right) teaches Taekwondo moves to a student. The CIA was created in 1947, and recruited many staff from the OSS, which had worked with resistance groups during World War II.

Part of a team

Spies out in the field on a mission can appear to have a lonely job, but in many cases, they are not alone. They are supported by a dedicated team of operatives, from specialists in break-ins, to bugging and surveillance officers, all of whom depend on each other for the success of their mission, and sometimes even their lives. This team is, in turn, part of a far larger network of secret service staff working on a particular operation.

▶ This scene depicts a mission for the fictional XYZ secret service. A defector has identified someone who will work as a mole for the XYZ. A double agent working for the XYZ meets with the mole to receive top secret documents. At the same time, another unit is searching and bugging the mole's hotel room.

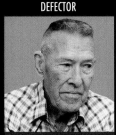

In a safehouse, a newly rented apartment is checked in advance for bugs. A case officer in charge of the mission interrogates the defector for further information.

The cryptologist specializes in cracking the codes used in the documents delivered by the courier. Once translated, the documents will be sent to the secret service headquarters.

The intelligence cycle

Gathering intelligence may be the work of spies out in the field, but it is only part of a long process known as the intelligence cycle. This begins with senior figures deciding precisely what intelligence is needed, planning how to obtain it and, once collected, analyzing the recovered information to produce reports. Vast amounts of intelligence are collected by staff who never enter the field. Instead, they use computers and communications links to monitor open sources – sources of information which are freely available such as foreign newspapers or radio broadcasts.

Large numbers

Although a well-kept secret, a large secret service such as the CIA or SVR is thought to employ over 15,000 people. Many work as translators or linguists, computer or communications specialists, or they are analysts in a specific area, such as a particular region of the world. Others are highly skilled technicians in trades such as printing or electronics engineering, and are able to provide spies in the field with the documents, clothing or equipment they need. Secret service staff also work in the fields of counter-surveillance, sweeping buildings to locate bugs, for example, and counter-espionage, seeking out enemy spies and activities in their own country and secret service.

DEFECTOR

A defector is a member of an intelligence agency who flees and gives vital information to the secret service of another country, and often receives asylum in return. In 1985, Oleg Gordievsky (1938–) went out for a jog from his apartment in Moscow, but in fact defected from the former Soviet Union to Britain, where he identified a number of Soviets living in Britain as spies.

DOUBLE AGENT

A double agent spies for two or more rival intelligence services. On many occasions, he or she pretends to be loyal to the original masters while actually spying on them for another service. One of the most successful double agents was the Spaniard Juan Pujol (1912–1988), who fed the Germans false information during World War II when he worked for British intelligence.

MOLE

Moles are enemy agents who infiltrate a rival security service and work there, digging out valuable information for another country's secret service. In 1965, Karl F Koecher (1934–) appeared to defect from Czechoslovakia (now the Czech Republic) to the USA to work for the CIA as a translator. He was, in fact, a mole for the Czech secret service until his detection in 1984.

While the meeting takes place in the park, a break-in technician gains entry to the mole's hotel room, where a search is carried out.

The electronics technician lays a phone tap and hidden sound-recording bugs in the hotel room.

Hidden from view, a surveillance officer monitors the meeting in the park using high-powered binoculars. He may document the meeting with photographs.

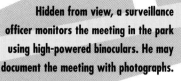

Some time after the meeting in the park has finished, a courier collects the documents and ferries them across town to a cryptologist, a specialist in breaking the foreign security service's codes.

The double agent collects information left by the mole and leaves it discreetly at a dead drop site to be collected by a courier.

The mole meets the double agent at night at an agreed location, a quiet park.

CASE OFFICER

Case officers frequently plan and run local missions. Some recruit and run spies who work out in the field, and are sometimes known as handlers. Victor I Cherkashin (c.1932–) was a case officer for the KGB who worked out of the Soviet embassy in Washington DC. Cherkashin handled some of the KGB's most valuable American spies, such as Robert Hanssen (see page 33).

SURVEILLANCE OFFICER

Members of a surveillance team must be undetectable to the targets they are observing. They may be specialists in sound gathering, visual observation or electronic monitoring. Some work alone, tailing a suspect, others in teams, staking out a location. FBI vehicle surveillance officers are nicknamed 'wheel artists', and use various tactics to avoid detection.

BREAK-IN EXPERT

Break-in (surreptitious entry) experts help gain access to locked, guarded or alarmed places. A key or electronic door card may be stolen and quickly duplicated, or locks picked and alarms disabled. While working as a valet for the British ambassador in Turkey during World War II, German spy Elyesa Bazna (1904–1970) made wax impressions of keys to locked document boxes.

ELECTRONICS TECHNICIAN

Secret services employ many field specialists, including electronic surveillance technicians, who are experts at planting bugs and tapping phones, using devices often developed by technical officers back at headquarters. Peter Wright (1916–1995) was a pioneer technical officer for MI5 who invented many of the bugs and taps used by British intelligence agencies.

COURIER

Couriers ferry documents, information and objects out of a danger area and into the hands of a secret service. They often work as a link between an agent and his or her case officer or handler. A courier's work is very dangerous and they are often considered expendable. French SOE operative Andrée Borrel (1919–1944) was an SOE agent and courier until her capture by the Germans.

CRYPTOLOGIST

Cryptologists are specialists in the analysis, breaking and making of codes. William and Elizabeth Friedman (both 1891–1969) worked as expert cryptologists in both world wars. During World War II, William Friedman was part of the US team that broke the Purple machine code used by Japan to send its top secret messages.

Recruiting spies

What makes someone want to become a spy? The work can be long, hard and desperately dangerous, while the glory for performing a successful mission can be shared only with a tiny handful of secret service colleagues. Despite the risks, people of all ages and backgrounds have become spies. Some are attracted by the thrill and sense of adventure, others by flattery, money or their beliefs. Some are forced into spying through blackmail or deception.

Riches and rewards

Many of the world's spies have been motivated solely or in part by the lure of large sums of money in return for their spying. A secret service's recruiting officers may approach a highly placed politician, military officer or member of another secret service if background checks reveal they have got themselves into financial difficulties. Other people volunteer their services, and information they can secure, to secret services for a price. In 1985, debt-ridden senior CIA officer Aldrich Ames (1941–) left a note at the Soviet embassy offering his services in return for money. Until his capture in 1994, Ames was paid more than one million pounds for information on over 90 secret CIA operations and the identities of an estimated 30 undercover spies.

◀ Recruiting officers skilfully play on a potential new recruit's beliefs, personality and weaknesses, earning their trust and using flattery, money and sometimes threats to get them to take the final steps to becoming a spy.

Deception and blackmail

Some spies are duped into spying through trickery or are forced to spy through deception, threats or blackmail. Secret services set up blackmail traps, such as using male or female operatives to seduce a target – people with access to secrets a country wants. Sometimes 'false flag deception' is used to make a potential recruit believe they will be working for a secret service they agree with, when in fact their intelligence is going to a quite different agency.

Targets are identified, evaluated and their background, personality, lifestyle and contacts thoroughly checked. This research can bring up a secret from the target's past which can be used for blackmail purposes. West German MP Alfred Frenzel (1899–1968) was blackmailed by the Czech StB. Approaching Frenzel in 1956, the StB threatened to reveal his past as a member of the Czech Communist Party and his criminal record, revelations which would damage, possibly ruin, his political career. As a member of the parliamentary defence committee, Frenzel had access to many top secret documents which he passed on to the Czechs, including a complete copy of the defence budget, and details of new military aircraft to be stationed in West Germany.

◀ The majority of staff who work for a secret service are recruited in the typical ways that most people get jobs. Many intelligence agency positions are advertised as major organizations often sponsor some students through further education.

Spying for one's beliefs

Many spies, especially in wartime, spy for their own country in the belief that they are simply doing their duty. British author Somerset Maugham (1874–1965), for example, spied for British intelligence in Switzerland and Russia during World War I, and did the work unpaid, believing it was his patriotic duty. Others, disillusioned with their country, or firm followers of a certain religion or political philosophy, often spy for services which share those views, as was the case with the communism-supporting Cambridge spies (see page 30).

Agnes Smedley (1892–1950), for instance, began spying for Indian nationalists after she became a firm supporter for India gaining independence from Britain. She later went on to spy for communist Chinese and Soviet interests.

▼ Alfred Frenzel, known to his Czech spymasters as Codename Anna, is escorted into a West German court after his capture in October 1960. The following year he received a 15-year prison sentence but, in 1966, he was returned to Czechoslovakia in exchange for four West German spies.

Spy rings

Individual spies are sometimes part of a small collection of fellow agents using some of the same facilities and couriers or reporting to the same handlers. These groups are often called spy rings or networks. Heading the activities of spy rings are spymasters. They wield enormous influence in their security service and, in some countries, their government as well.

▼ Anthony Blunt (left) as an undergraduate at Cambridge University, where he was recruited to work as a Soviet spy. Blunt's role as the fourth man in the Cambridge Spy Ring was only made public in 1979.

The man with no face

Markus Wolf (1923–) is considered one of the greatest spymasters of the 20th century. Working for East Germany, his identity was kept a secret from the West for more than 20 years, earning him the nickname 'the man with no face'. Wolf proved highly skilled at recruiting and working with moles in rival secret services and foreign governments. Wolf's greatest coup was placing an agent, Gunter Guillaume (1927–1995), into the heart of the West German government. In 1970, Guillaume became a personal advisor to the West German chancellor, Willy Brandt (1913–1992), and had access to the highest level secret government documents, which he copied and passed back to East Germany. Guillaume's closeness to government was such that within a month of his capture in 1974, Brandt resigned as West German leader.

▲ Legendary East German spymaster Markus Wolf ran East Germany's HVA from the mid-1950s until his retirement in 1987.

The Cambridge spies

In the 1930s, the Soviet Union recruited many British and American students at Cambridge University, England. Amongst them were Guy Burgess (1911–1963), Anthony Blunt (1907–1983), Donald Maclean (1913–1983) and Kim Philby (1912–1988). All four men went on to take senior positions in the British government or the intelligence services. Maclean became a senior diplomat and worked in Washington DC, USA, with access to documents about atomic weapons and other crucial secrets. Burgess worked at MI6 during World War II and also worked in Washington DC after the war. Meanwhile, Kim Philby was so successful in British intelligence that in 1946 he was put in charge of MI6's counter-espionage operations. This allowed him to betray British and American missions to the KGB. In 1951, with British spycatchers closing in, Philby tipped off Burgess and Maclean, who both defected to the Soviet Union. With suspicions aroused, Philby resigned from his post and also defected. The rumours of both a fourth and a fifth man in the spy ring proved accurate many years later with the unmasking of Anthony Blunt and John Cairncross (1913–1995).

The atomic spies

A major spy ring operated in the USA during and after World War II. Its goal was to obtain the vital secrets of the US atomic bomb programme, known during the war as 'the Manhattan Project', and to transfer it to the Soviet Union. The ring, which included scientists involved in the Manhattan Project, was ultimately successful and saved the Soviet Union many years of painstaking research. But the spies paid the price with many years in prison. In the case of two of the atomic spies, Julius (1918–1953) and Ethel Rosenberg (1915–1953), they paid with their lives, as they were sentenced to death in twin electric chairs.

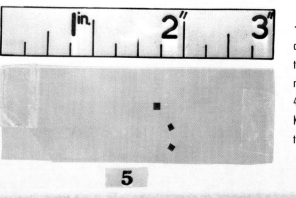

◄ Magnified one and a half times, these three secret microdots (see page 45) were found in the Krogers' possession at their house in Ruislip.

The Portland spies

An unassuming bungalow in London's surburbia proved to be the base of a major spy ring run by spymaster Gordon Lonsdale, aka Konon Molody (1924–1970). His spies gained access to large numbers of top secret documents relating to Britain's military submarine programme. Many of these secrets were sent to Moscow via radio transmissions from the house in Ruislip. Searches there revealed a secret cellar, microdot reader and even a KGB expenses form. The couple who lived there, the Krogers, ran an antique books business, but were actually KGB agents under deep cover. Although Molody, the Krogers and two other spies were arrested and imprisoned, to this day no one is certain how many more agents were part of Molody's spy ring.

▲ Ethel Gee returns home in 1970 after serving nine years of her 15-year prison sentence as part of the Portland spy ring. Gee worked at the Underwater Detection Establishment at Portland, England, and passed on many naval military secrets.

► Kim Philby relaxes in exile at a Russian resort bordering the Black Sea. Philby held a senior post in MI6, and was thought of as a possible future head of the secret service before he resigned his post and finally defected to the Soviet Union in 1963.

Spycatching

Spies live in fear of surveillance, detection and, ultimately, capture. This fear rarely subsides when an undetected spy retires. For example, Robert S Lipka (1946–) spied for the Soviet Union's KGB while he worked for America's NSA in the 1960s. He was arrested in 1996, 22 years after his very last contact with his KGB spymasters. Spycatching is a major part of a secret service's work and most have entire sections of their service, called counter-espionage or counter-intelligence, devoted to this task.

▲ Arthur James Walker is led from court by an FBI agent in 1985. Recruited by his younger brother, John Walker, to obtain US military secrets for the KGB, the Walker spy ring was uncovered after a tip-off from John Walker's ex-wife.

Betrayed

Routine checks, surveillance and lie detector (polygraph) tests are commonplace in secret services. While these may catch some spies, most operatives are caught because someone identified and betrayed them.

Defectors, double agents and moles often uncover details of spies in a secret service. In 1959, a senior Polish intelligence officer told the CIA about two Soviet agents operating in Britain, one of whom was uncovering British submarine secrets. The resultant investigation led to the capture in 1961 of the Portland spies (see page 31).

A small number of spies have been unmasked by friends or family members or vigilant secretaries. In Soviet spy Rudolf Abel's (1903–1971) case, it was an American paperboy to whom he had mistakenly given his five cent coin, hollowed out to carry secret messages.

Making mistakes

Spies make mistakes. Sometimes, they are simply not careful enough, using the same dead drop sites, confiding their identity to someone or not checking for bugs or surveillance.

◀ This trunk was used in 1964 to ferry captured Israeli double agent Mordecai Louk back to Egypt after he had been caught by the Egyptian secret service. Louk was drugged and his hands, head and feet bound inside the trunk. A delay at an Italian airport thwarted the plan as Louk's shouts alerted Italian custom officials.

Other spies foolishly flaunt their new-found wealth. This was the case with industrial spy Dr Ronald Hoffman (see page 19) whose luxurious lifestyle – that included a luxury yacht – as a company scientist, aroused suspicion.

The next step

Once a spy is identified, a secret service has a number of options. Some spies are identified, without their knowing, and left to continue work, but are fed false information or are heavily tracked in the hope of uncovering a spy ring or more senior spies. Spies who are caught are usually interrogated to discover what they know. This interrogation, which in some countries involves threats and torture, can lead to unmasking other spies, their handler or case officer or an entire spy ring. Some captured spies are turned against their original masters to become double agents but most are 'neutralized': in many countries today, this means a court trial and imprisonment if found guilty. In some cases, a captured spy faces execution.

TO CATCH A SPY

One of the KGB's most damaging spies in the USA was finally captured in 2001. Robert Phillip Hanssen (1944–) was an FBI agent for 27 years, but for over half of those years, he had worked for the KGB. Starting in 1979, Hanssen supplied the KGB with thousands of pages of documents which betrayed at least four double agents and compromised many US spying operations. The CIA obtained documents from one of Hanssen's Soviet contacts. Spycatchers sometimes have to convert suspicions into proof, collecting enough evidence to show without doubt, that the person under investigation is a hostile spy. Here is the abbreviated story of Robert Hanssen's surveillance and capture.

FBI SUSPECT HANSSEN! They promote him so they can monitor his movements...

UNDERCOVER AGENTS WATCH HANSSEN'S HOUSE IN TALISMAN DRIVE.

THE FBI BUG AND SEARCH HANSSEN'S CAR.

Hanssen's handheld computer reveals his plans for a dead drop on 18 February.

DEAD DROP ON 18 FEBRUARY

THE FBI TAP HANSSEN'S PHONE... and listen in on his calls.

18 FEBRUARY – THE DEAD DROP! The FBI watch Hanssen transfer a floppy disk and stolen FBI files into a bin bag.

THE FBI TRAIL HANSSEN TO THE DEAD DROP SITE. Hanssen places the bin bag on a rusty beam beneath the footbridge over Wolftrap Creek, Foxstone Park, USA.

THE FBI HAVE PROOF AT LAST! They arrest Hanssen.

HANSSEN'S WIFE DRIVES TO DULLES AIRPORT TO MEET HER HUSBAND AS ARRANGED. She is seized by FBI agents and interrogated for eight hours.

HANSSEN IS SENTENCED IN COURT TO LIFE IMPRISONMENT WITHOUT PAROLE...

SUMMARY OF CHAPTER 2: SPIES AND SECRET SERVICES

Compact, reliable pistols are popular with security agencies worldwide.

Who do spies work for?

Some spies operate alone, occasionally surfacing to sell their secrets or services to the highest bidder. Most spies, however, work for one or more of the world's secret services. These are organizations which gather and supply intelligence to their governments. Secret services spy on people within their own country and abroad.

What is a spy ring?

A spy ring is the nickname given to a relatively small number of spies all working together or all recruited or handled by one spymaster. Spy rings can contain just two or three people or dozens of agents.

Why do people become spies?

There are many reasons that people become spies, including the thrill or excitement a person feels at doing the work, or large sums of money they may be paid for secrets. Some spy for a country or cause they believe in, or spy against a country or cause they are strongly against. Other spies are recruited by a secret service which uses blackmail, threats and deception against them.

How are spies caught?

Sometimes spies give themselves up, but often spies are caught because someone betrays their identity. Counter-intelligence branches of secret services hunt out spies using spying techniques including surveillance, phone-tapping and bugging. Some spies have been caught because they have not been careful enough, or their spending habits and behaviour have prompted investigation by a government agency.

Go further...

 Visit the KGB Museum in Moscow online:
www.fsb.ru/eng/history/museum.html

Learn more about the British secret service, MI5:
www.mi5.gov.uk

Find out about the top secret successes of the KGB during the Cold War:
www.pbs.org/redfiles/kgb/index.htm

Check out *Eye Spy* magazine's online news and features sections:
www.eyespymag.com

Learn more about the activities of the CIA at their official website:
www.cia.gov

 Vetting investigations officer
Interviews and assesses potential candidates for employment in a security service.

Polygraph officer
Administers lie-detecting tests and analyzes the results to screen security service recruits, existing staff members, suspects or double agents.

Mobile surveillance officer
Observes and tracks suspected double agents and other targets.

Political analyst
Assesses intelligence and researches to understand the intentions of governments or groups in a region.

 Find out more about the evasion techniques and weapons used during the world wars and Cold War.
Imperial War Museum North
The Quays
Trafford Wharf
Manchester M17 1TZ
Telephone: +44 (0) 161 836 4000
www.iwm.org.uk/north/index.htm

Visit the concrete labyrinth which would have been home to regional and military command for northwest England if nuclear war had broken out during the Cold War.
Hack Green Nuclear Bunker
PO Box 127
Nantwich
Telephone: +44 (0) 1270 629219
www.hackgreen.co.uk

CHAPTER 3

Techniques and equipment

The world's earliest spies used their eyes and memory to assist them in intelligence gathering. Over time, a range of spying techniques, such as disguise, code systems and surveillance, was developed, as were essential spying tools such as lockpicks and false identities.

The tools and skills involved in spying greatly increased in the 20th century CE with the arrival of practical photography, aerial and satellite observation, radio communications and computers. But modern spies never forget that their enemies may have similar capabilities.

◀ A US paratrooper approaches his landing site
during the Vietnam War (1965–1975). Spies working
in hostile territory may parachute in, be dropped ashore
stealthily by boat or occasionally are smuggled hidden in
the boot of a car, crates, barrels or some other container.

Breaking in – getting out

To succeed in his or her mission, a spy needs to gain entry to compounds, buildings, vehicles and other locations. Guards and guard dogs may be drugged or killed, burglar alarms dismantled and the codes for coded entry points cracked. Lock-picking and safe-cracking techniques are frequently employed. A spy then finds a way of leaving the mission site, but if caught, he or she may use concealed equipment such as a pepper gas spray to escape.

Gaining entry

Secret services employ specialists with the skills to find a way into secure places. In many situations, a specialist equipped with lock-picking tools is able to get past mechanical and electronic locks in less than ten minutes. But when gaining access is less straightforward, planning is required. Detailed building plans may reveal a route in using service tunnels, sewers or ventilation shafts. A security guard may be tricked so that spies can duplicate a key or smartcard. Other missions may call for a spy to bluff their way in with a suitable disguise.

Escape and evasion

Mission completed, spies try to melt away unnoticed, sometimes adopting a disguise or hiding until their route is safe. Some spies are instructed to pass on their vital data immediately, or there may be an elaborate series of fake dead drops or meetings with decoy couriers to take enemy surveillance off the scent. From the early 1980s onwards, the CIA issued some agents with an ingenious device called a jib. This was a rapidly inflating dummy human which could be used to replace a spy inside a car shortly after the real agent had rolled out and escaped.

▼ A spectacular getaway from the 2002 James Bond movie, *Die Another Day*. In contrast to fictional spies such as James Bond, real-life agents seek to make a quiet and anonymous exit from their mission site, arousing as little suspicion or alarm as possible.

Operation Noah's Ark

Spies often have to escape with equipment that is unusual or difficult to conceal. Mossad's audacious mission in 1969, codenamed Operation Noah's Ark, called on its spies to escape with five gunboats from the French port of Cherbourg. Israel had paid for the ships, but a French arms embargo prevented their release. A number of 'Norwegian' sailors started work in the French port. Some of these sailors were Israeli spies. On Christmas Eve night, the vessels were sailed secretly back to Israel.

▲ This circuit-board micro-camera, complete with microphone attached by a cable, can be fitted into electrical goods or household objects so that it is unnoticeable.

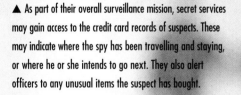

▲ As part of their overall surveillance mission, secret services may gain access to the credit card records of suspects. These may indicate where the spy has been travelling and staying, or where he or she intends to go next. They also alert officers to any unusual items the suspect has bought.

Surveillance

Surveillance is the planned observation of a target over a period of time. It is used to gain intelligence about a military force, rival agency or suspected spy, to discover possible blackmail targets, and to check out an individual's cover story. Surveillance targets can also be places. A team may set up posts around an enemy safehouse, for instance. Hidden cameras, electronic bugs, sound recorders and tracking devices fitted to a target's vehicle, are all common surveillance tools.

Tailing and tracking

Surveillance officers often work as part of a team which can include operatives involved in a stakeout at a fixed location. The team may also include mobile officers who tail their target on foot or in vehicles. Staying undetected requires training and teamwork. On foot, agents may work in units with one handing over surveillance to another if detected. On the roads, the FBI surveillance teams, for example, often use a number of different types of vehicle to form a 'floating box' which 'surrounds' the target vehicle and travels with it while staying undetected.

In addition, small tracking devices can be fitted to the underside of vehicles which, using radio or global positioning systems, can pinpoint the target vehicle's location and movement.

▲ This tiny transmitter is small enough to be planted almost anywhere without being detected. Spies fit similar bugs to everyday items, such as spectacles.

◄ Small, everyday items such as this matching pen and pocket calculator can be bought containing miniature bugs that transmit conversations and other sounds. That means anyone can practise the art of surveillance.

Spy dust

The KGB is believed to have used a tracking system from the 1960s onwards known as 'spy dust'. This was a harmless chemical compound which was placed on door knobs and other places so that only the people who had entered the room or touched the object would carry the chemical on them. Using an infrared light source, the KGB surveillance agents were able to detect and track the movements of these people.

Today, a similar powder, detectable only by using a UV (ultraviolet) light, is commercially available. It can be placed on the backs of vehicles for night surveillance or used to identify who last handled a document.

Cameras and surveillance

Cameras are a vital tool in collecting surveillance information. Spies might use powerful zoom lenses to shoot pictures from 100m away, or use footage obtained from CCTV cameras (see pages 20–21) or micro-cameras hidden in everyday objects such as bags. Copy cameras have been used for many decades to make reproductions of top secret documents, allowing the originals to be left in place.

Avoiding surveillance

Experienced spies seek to outwit surveillance by losing an enemy observer, sweeping rooms for bugs and hidden cameras, and by making last minute changes to travel and accommodation plans. A spy who suspects he or she is being observed may interrupt the mission by going to a secret signal site. This is a location agreed in advance where a spy or case officer can leave some sort of sign, as simple as a piece of dropped litter or a chalk mark, which lets a colleague know of the change of plan.

▼ Positioned on a balcony above a street, a surveillance team keeps watch and photographs its target zone below, which could be the entrance to a building, a suspected dead drop site or a meeting point for two spies.

Eye spy

Watching your enemies, knowing their positions and equipment and being able to track their movements are essential elements of intelligence gathering. Spies make use of many viewing aids such as telescopes, binoculars and single eyepiece monoculars. More recently, the invention of advanced thermal imagers, image intensifiers and night vision equipment means that spies can work better at night than before. Soaring high over agents in the field are spy planes carrying ground sensors and high resolution cameras, while hundreds of kilometres above them orbit satellites, spying on the land and sea below.

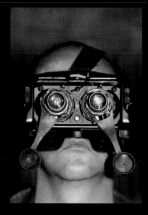

▲ Night vision goggles worn on the head keep an agent's hands free while providing him or her with a view at night, in misty conditions or inside a dark building.

Zooming in

Being able to see a target clearly is vital to achieving success in all sorts of missions, from surveillance and spycatching to assassination or breaking into a dark building. Spies are less at risk of detection or capture if they gather visual information from long distances, hundreds of metres away from the target. More than 25 countries use spy planes to conduct aerial reconnaissance over hostile territory. The USA has the biggest fleet of spy planes while China, Russia and France all have large numbers. Spy plane cameras have revealed build-ups of armed forces along the borders of many countries. They have also enabled analysts to spot new missile sites (Cuban Missile Crisis, see pages 8–9) or other weapons facilities, and to monitor the progress of a particular convoy or a town or factory's rebuilding. Spy planes are frequently unarmed, relying on sheer speed and high altitudes for safety. The recently retired Lockheed SR71 Blackbird spy plane, for example, remains the world's fastest jet aircraft, with a maximum speed of 3,200km/h.

Spying from space

Spy satellites first appeared in the 1960s, and have now taken over much of the work of spy planes. In 1999, *Ikonos II*, the world's first high resolution satellite owned by a private company, was launched into orbit 680km above earth. From that great distance, it can take photos revealing objects on the ground as small as 1m across. The information remains top secret, but modern spy satellites operated by countries may have even greater viewing abilities. For example, it is known that at least three of the USA's spy satellites run by the NRO are keyhole-class devices, able to detect and see objects as small as 10cm in diameter. The USA plans to spend over 16 billion pounds in the next 20 years to develop even more powerful spy satellites. On the ground, huge advances in computers and software mean that detailed 3D scenes of restricted areas, such as a rival power's military compounds, can be produced. Created using satellite images, photos taken from the ground and other data such as building plans, these 3D scenes enable agents to plan and train for top secret missions.

◀ Thermal imagers generate clear views in poor light conditions by collecting and amplifying the infrared energy emitted from objects. This thermal image shows an intruder climbing some railings. Because they require no light to illuminate the scene, thermal imagers are not detectable themselves. This makes them excellent for undercover work.

▶ The green-tinged picture from this image intensifier comes from the device's phosphor screen, which amplifies the available light to give a spy a form of night vision. An image intensifier's screen is coloured green because the human eye can differentiate more shades of green than any other phosphor colour. Image intensifiers for the military and spies often feature a light-secure eyeguard. This is a device which shuts off the phosphor screen when an agent's eye is not pressed up to the eyepiece, to prevent the tell-tale green glow giving away their position. The soldier in this picture is also wearing an image intensifier.

Listening in

People have been listening secretly to other people's conversations for centuries, but the equipment used to perform this task today is highly sophisticated. To record conversations, spies carry tiny digital voice recorders hidden in pens or clothing. They can point sophisticated directional microphones to pick up a conversation from a safe distance away without being seen, and they can monitor conversations from hundreds of metres away using high-tech electronic eavesdropping gadgets.

Bugging the enemy

A bug is a hidden microphone. It can be attached to a tape recorder by an electric cable, or to a radio transmitter that relays the sounds it collects to a receiver some distance away. Phone taps are a type of bug installed on a phone or communications line that enable spies to listen to conversations. Secret services have developed many ingenious ways of hiding bugs so that they are hard to detect. Electronic surveillance teams often bug a government building that is being renovated. Bugs are fitted inside walls, fixtures and fittings. The KGB fitted at least 40 bugs when the US embassy in Moscow was renovated in the 1950s.

▼ East German officials examine some of the equipment left behind when the CIA's Berlin tunnel was abandoned in 1956. The 400m-long tunnel, dug into East German territory, was used to tap into important enemy communications lines for some 14 months. Every day, 600 tape recorders in the tunnel recorded 1,200 hours of material, which was flown back to the USA for analysis.

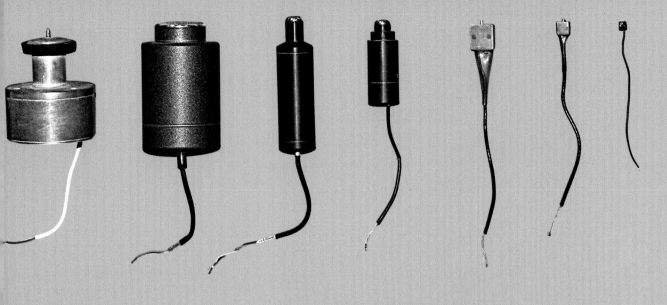

◄ This selection of bugs from the International Spy Museum in Washington DC, USA, spans 50 years from World War II (far left) through the decades to the late 1990s (far right). Over time, smaller and smaller bugs have been built, and spies have found ever more creative ways of hiding them.

Good vibrations

Leon Theremin (1896–1993) is famous for the pioneering electronic instrument which bears his surname and was used on songs such as the Beach Boys' *Good Vibrations*. But he also invented a simple yet effective bugging device which required no power source and transmitted no radio signals, making it very hard to detect. The device, dubbed 'The Thing', was fitted into a replica of the Great Seal of the USA that was given as a gift by the Soviet Union. It hung on a wall in the office of the US Ambassador to Moscow for over six years before it was detected. The device worked by radio waves being transmitted towards it from a van outside the embassy. These radio waves bounced back to the van from The Thing complete with sounds.

A cat and mouse game

A constant battle rages between secret service teams that place bugs and taps and other teams that hunt for bugs and taps. A range of electronic devices exists with which agents can 'sweep' a room to detect unusual radio signals. Tracing a phone tap can be more difficult, as a spy can place a tap anywhere between the phone receiver and the telephone exchange. Many secure phone calls are made using a device called a scrambler, which breaks up the sound signal into lots of random segments before it is transmitted down a phone line. The receiver's phone must be equipped with the same scrambling device for the call to be pieced back together.

► Global telecommunications rely on satellite transmitting and receiving dishes. Some secret services have the capability to intercept and eavesdrop on satellite communications.

◄ US Ambassador Henry Cabot Lodge Jr. displays the Great Seal, containing The Thing bug, to the United Nations Security Council in 1960. The bug was placed behind a small opening on the carved eagle's beak.

▲ Many everyday items, such as this wine cork, can be hollowed out to make a secret message compartment.

Getting a message back

Spies may locate top secret papers or microfilm but the mission is far from over. They still have to get this vital intelligence back to base and must use various means at their disposal, including the use of a courier or a hidden message. But the developments in photography, radio communications and computing have increased the options.

Couriers and cut outs

Many messages and documents have to be moved physically from place to place. Couriers (see pages 26–27) are often used to transport information and messages which may be coded, written in invisible ink or hidden in some way. Some couriers never know the identity of the spy who supplies them with the intelligence they are to transport, or even the people who will receive the information. Some couriers serve as a cut out, allowing communication between a spy and his or her case officer without them meeting. Homing pigeons and dogs have served as couriers, as have people who were unaware that they were carrying a message smuggled in their luggage.

◄ This 1906 postcard carries no codes or invisible ink, just a message seemingly from someone seeking a British penpal. However, the card was sent by an unnamed British intelligence officer and the photograph depicts the German naval fleet in Kiel Harbour.

Invisible ink

Invisible ink may seem the stuff of James Bond films, but it has a long history in real-life spying. Lemon juice and urine are two liquids which appear invisible on a page but reappear when heated. In the 20th century CE, a variety of new invisible inks and special papers were invented which required bathing in special chemicals to reveal their message. Other invisible inks become visible only when UV light is shone on the paper. When German spy Oswald Job's (1885–1944) letters were intercepted during World War II, they appeared to be innocent notes to friends in France. It was only when they were sent to an MI5 laboratory that intelligence messages to German forces were revealed written in invisible ink.

◄ Spies who are not undercover may make use of mobile phones to communicate with others, but there are risks, as it is possible for security services to tap into mobile phone calls.

► A dead drop site is a place agreed in advance where a transfer of information, messages, money or equipment takes place without the two parties meeting. This dead drop spike is a waterproof metal cylinder into which a roll of film or a document can be placed. The spike is pressed into the ground for collection later.

▼ Played on a normal cassette player, this audio tape may carry a song, but played on an adapted machine, it reveals a hidden message.

► This female Belgian courier for the Germans is shown shortly before she was executed for spying during World War I. She carried a secret message written on her back in invisible ink.

Steganography

Hiding messages and information is a practice called steganography. Many ingenious methods have been used for centuries. For example, during the Greek wars against Persia almost 2,500 years ago, a messenger's head was shaved, a secret message written on his scalp and the hair allowed to re-grow. Messages have been secreted inside almost every object imaginable, from talcum powder tins to the backs of postage stamps. Hidden messages can still be discovered by accident, which is why most are also encrypted (see pages 46–47) for extra security. Microdot photography can reduce a document down in size more than 300 times. A microdot of this page would be smaller than a full stop, but could be read with a microscope.

Codes and ciphers

Spies, governments and military forces all require secrecy and security when sending important messages. They turn to the science of code- and cipher-making, which is known as cryptography or cryptology. A code is a 'secret language' used to disguise a message by replacing words, phrases or sentences with different groups of letters, numbers or symbols. A cipher is a type of code which conceals a message by scrambling its letters.

▼ Two native American Navajo code talkers transmit military intelligence during World War II. The Navajo code talkers served with various US Marine units and devised a code based on their language, which the Japanese were unable to break.

Codes through the ages

Codes and ciphers have been used throughout history. In 405BCE, Lysander of Sparta (unknown–395BCE) received a secret message written on the inside of a servant's belt. The belt had to be wound around a wooden staff of a certain thickness for the letters in the belt to line up to spell out the message that a Persian general was about to attack. The arrival of wireless communications, such as radio, which are more easily intercepted than physical messages, such as letters, intensified the battle between code-makers and breakers. The breaking of the code used on the Zimmerman telegram (1917), for instance, played a major part in the outcome of World War I.

◀ While pretending to be a butterfly collector, British spy Lord Baden-Powell (1857–1941) successfully surveyed an enemy fortress in the Balkans in 1890. He disguised his drawings of the fortification (shown in red) as veins in the wings of sketches of butterflies. Spots on the wings showed the positions of artillery guns.

The Enigma Code

Before and during World War II, Germany used a modified and improved Enigma code-making machine to create what it believed were unbreakable codes. The Enigma machine was impressive, the later versions being capable of encoding a message in 159 trillion different ways. British code-breaking efforts were centred around a dedicated team at Bletchley Park, England, under the codename 'Ultra'. The team was helped greatly by Polish resistance workers who managed to ferry a captured Enigma machine to Britain as well as by the drawings and work of Polish code experts from the 1930s. Despite the Germans changing the codes on a daily basis, the Ultra team was able to intercept and break as many as 2,000 signals or messages a day, while the Germans still believed the Enigma code remained secret.

Going digital

Some of the earliest computers were devoted to code-breaking during World War II. Since that time, computers have revolutionized code- and cipher-making and breaking. Sensitive computer data is protected by software while secret services have centres using powerful supercomputers to analyze codes and to create new, more secure ones.

▶ Out in the field, two female US intelligence officers intercept wireless communications which may contain vital encrypted messages.

Disguise and cover

Spies rarely like to stand out in a crowd. The aim of many spies' disguises is to blend in with the people and surroundings of their mission area. When backed with a cover story, forged identity papers and knowledge of the local language and customs, a good disguise can enable a spy to travel without attracting attention. But disguises are also adopted for other purposes. When on surveillance missions or threatened with surveillance themselves, a spy may seek to change their identity in mid-mission to avoid being spotted. Spies may also use a disguise to fool someone who knows them into not recognizing their real identity.

◄ By wearing an oversized suit, the spy appears as an overweight, middle-aged businessman, hailing a taxi. His padded stomach may be a strapped-on bag containing another complete disguise.

► Simple changes of clothes, along with alterations in voice, body language and attitude, can enable an agent (centre image) to travel unnoticed, obtain access to a target or protected area, or make their escape stealthily without detection.

Much more than make-up

Using make-up and props, a spy can dramatically alter his or her facial appearance by appearing to age greatly, or by changing nationality or even gender. Many female spies have succeeded in disguising themselves as men to avoid suspicion or detection. During the US Civil War, a white woman, Emma Edmonds (c.1840–1898), acted as a spy for the Union forces, dyeing her skin and wearing a wig to successfully disguise herself as a black male slave. Changing facial appearance can be important but is only part of an effective disguise. Spies also perfect different styles of walking, gestures and body language.

▲ Film star Johnny Depp is shown both cleanshaven and with a beard, hat and glasses. Elements of theatrical make-up and costume design are used by spies, to create completely convincing disguises.

► Dressed as a busy urban courier, the spy can pass unnoticed and gain access to buildings. Over a number of visits, disguised as a courier, the spy may gain an employee's trust or learn the access codes to the building.

► An old man shambling down the street attracts little attention. Here, the spy aims his walking stick, which contains a tranquillizer dart gun, in order to put a guard dog to sleep.

► By using easily available props and make-up, the spy has created a different facial disguise. A photo of the disguised spy may be used on fake identity cards or other official documents.

Quick-change artist

Often a disguise has to be put on quickly in an enclosed area, such as a toilet in a train carriage. Some spies carry essential disguise items, such as a mirror, basic make-up, fake facial hair and reversible clothing, which can be put on very quickly. Hats, glasses and sunglasses, and quick-colour hair dyes are all ways of altering a spy's appearance. Some inexperienced spies have been discovered because they continue to carry the same bag or luggage after disguising themselves. A good spy will bundle all his or her possessions into a spare bag of a quite different design to complete their disguise. In just a few minutes, a spy can emerge looking like a different person. When the spy adds a change in mannerisms and walking pattern, the transformation is complete and could buy a spy time to escape.

From covers to complete histories

Secret agents, especially those operating in dangerous territory, back their disguise with a cover story. This often involves a false name, business cards and identity papers, as well as a background story of where the spy lives and works. 'Pocket litter' – various small possessions, such as a family photo, and objects connected with the spy's fake job – are also carried to support their false identity. A spy backs his or her disguise and cover with views and actions which reinforce their identity. Former US Navy officer John Walker Jr. (1937–) appeared to be very anti-communist and was a member of various right-wing groups. Yet for over 15 years, Walker was one of the KGB's most valuable spies in the US. Cover stories can extend back many years, with complete false family histories and employment records. Spies with the most thorough cover stories are often referred to as being in 'deep cover'. A spy establishes deep cover by living in an enemy territory for a number of years before they start their spying activities.

► Dressed as a janitor in overalls, the spy can clean floors in a building while keeping his eyes and ears open for vital information such as the password to a protected area.

▲ Beards can alter the shape of a person's face and draw attention away from other prominent facial features. Here, film star Brad Pitt has grown a large beard which makes him look quite different.

The art of concealment

For a spy in enemy territory, concealment can be the difference between success or failure, escape or death. Concealment is the art of disguising equipment or documents. Spies use the natural spaces in items, such as the battery compartment of a personal stereo, to hide objects. Ingenious engineering can create undetectable space in surprisingly small objects such as coins, small batteries or jewellery. Concealment can be used to hide escape devices, microdots and messages in a spy's clothing. Larger objects, such as weapons, can be concealed in the false bottom of a bag or even in fake rocks.

Wartime concealment

Wartime resistance movements relied on the art of concealment. During World War II, the OSS constructed hollowed-out lumps of coal containing explosives for use in missions against Germany. To help POWs (prisoners of war) escape from their German captors, gramophone records were sent to POW camps which, when broken, revealed banknotes, maps or identity papers inside.

◀ Sometimes items are concealed on a target without that person knowing. In the 1960s and 1970s, the KGB would steal a target's shoes while he or she slept, and fit a small microphone and transmitter inside the heel so that they could monitor conversations. They would return the shoes before the target woke up.

Everyday objects

In 1960, a courier for the Czech StB, Franz Altman, was captured by the West German BfV. Amongst his possessions was a tin of baby milk powder which, when searched, revealed six rolls of film. The documents on these films led back to Alfred Frenzel (see page 28) and played a major part in Frenzel's conviction as a Czech spy. It was not an isolated incident. Using ordinary objects to hide extraordinary spying tools and messages has been commonplace for many decades. Tubes of toothpaste, tins of boot polish, clothes, shaving brushes and sealed cans of food have all been modified to hide items such as fake passports, maps, rolls of film or small weapons.

Key to the contents of the coat:
1. Rubber gloves prevent fingerprints
2. Lockpicking tools
3. PDA (personal digital assistant)
4. Pen containing hidden bug and transmitter
5. Handgun positioned to allow a quick draw
6. Bug receiver and recording device
7. Detailed map of the area
8. High resolution digital zoom camera
9. Mobile phone fitted with secure channel
10. Bottle containing tranquillizing chemicals
11. Metal dead drop spike

◀ Faking nature is a classic way of concealing a major spy tool. Constructed by the CIA, this fake tree stump conceals a large, solar-powered bug and transmitter. It was planted near a Soviet airbase in the early 1970s and is now an exhibit at the International Spy Museum.

Hidden away

Many pieces of hidden spy kit such as the bug in the tree stump (above) have to be operated remotely. Concealed surveillance cameras are a classic example. One of these cameras may be placed so that the lens peers out of a small opening in the side of a bag, the spine of a book, a belt buckle or the lapel of a jacket or coat. The agent takes pictures by pressing a remote shutter button which may be fitted to a bag handle or hidden inside a pocket. The hidden camera remains safely out of the target's sight at all times.

▲ This US silver dollar is, in fact, a secret store for microdots, coded messages or lethal poisons. Made from two separate dollar coins, it is opened by pressing the top of the eagle's left wing.

◀ Clothes for fieldwork are often tailored to provide as many as 25 hidden pockets and linings in which agents can store all the tools of their trade. The latest versions contain built-in piping to house wiring from electronic spy devices.

▼ Built by the KGB during the Cold War, this F21 camera is fitted to a fake umbrella handle and slips into its black umbrella cover (right). A small hole in the cover provides a secret opening for the camera lens.

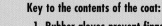

Secret weapons

Spies are often equipped with secret weapons designed to injure or kill a victim. Sometimes these weapons, such as concealed knives, poisonous gas sprays or miniature guns, are to aid a spy's escape. Others are a grim reminder that a spy may have to make the ultimate sacrifice and commit suicide if captured.

► This harmless-looking walking cane hides a needle in its tip, through which a pellet of lethal poison can be injected into a victim. It was developed by the KGB in the 1950s.

▼ Hidden easily in a pocket, bag or purse, the KGB's 'Kiss of Death' is a single-shot gun designed to look like a tube of lipstick.

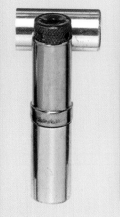

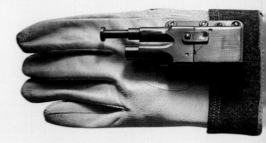

▲ This World War II secret weapon, designed for spies working for US naval intelligence, features a single-shot gun fitted to a leather glove and fired between the fingers.

Disguised but deadly

Secret weapons come in many guises. Some are designed for deliberate use by assassins (see pages 16–17). Others are to be used only in extreme circumstances, for example, if a mission is in danger of failing or a spy is threatened with capture. Garrottes – lengths of wire – are used to strangle victims, such as guards, silently. Knives and blades may be concealed in the heels of shoes, underneath the lapels of a jacket or coat, or inside a belt buckle. Miniature guns have been concealed in all sorts of everyday-looking items, from pens to pipes and cameras. In 1954, KGB assassin Nikolai Khokhlov (1922–) defected to West Germany. He carried with him an ingenious gun fitted inside a cigarette case which fired bullets tipped with poison.

Phone bombs

Bombs can be sent through the post, planted in a house or fitted inside or underneath a victim's car. In 1972, Mossad planned the phone bomb assassination of Dr Mhamood Alhamshari (unknown–1972), a senior official in the PLO. A Mossad assassin broke into his house and planted explosives inside his telephone. Once Alhamshari had returned home, the assassin rang the phone number and as Alhamshari lifted the handset, the bomb's detonator was triggered. Alhamshari died in hospital several days later. Mossad used the same technique with a mobile phone in 1996 to kill a suspected Palestinian terrorist, Yaya Ajash (unknown–1996).

Poisonous plans

Poisons can be hidden in rings, badges and buttons to be placed stealthily in a victim's food or drink. New lethal biological and chemical poisons are so powerful that only the tiniest amount needs to be swallowed or injected into the body to cause death. The CIA considered assassinating Cuban leader Fidel Castro (1927–), by contaminating a box of his cigars with the deadly botulism bacteria.

Fast-acting, lethal poisons are the most common way for spies to commit suicide. Some CIA agents, for example, were equipped with a poison-tipped pin hidden inside a hollowed silver dollar. One such 'dollar of death' was displayed at the Soviet trial of CIA pilot Gary Powers (see page 54).

▼ Worn over the fingers of a hand, this knuckleduster, made from aluminium, greatly increases the force of a punch.

The death of Georgi Markov

Bought in Washington DC, modified in Moscow and used in London, an ordinary black umbrella was converted into a deadly secret weapon injecting a pellet of ricin, a lethal and hard-to-trace poison. It was used to assassinate the exiled Bulgarian playwright and journalist Georgi Markov (1929–1978), who was an outspoken critic of the Communist government in Bulgaria. On 7 September 1978, Markov was heading for a bus stop on Waterloo Bridge when he felt a sharp pain in the back of his right thigh. He turned to see a man pick up an umbrella and quickly leave the scene in a taxi. The assassin had injected ricin through the sharpened tip of the umbrella. Markov went to work but the pain increased and he was taken to hospital that night. He died four days later. The assassin has never been traced.

Swapping spies and information

Sometimes the governments of two countries agree to exchange or trade vital intelligence. On other occasions, POWs and captured agents are also exchanged by nations. Spy swaps are carefully arranged, often after many months of negotiation. Trading of spies only occurs, however, if both sides believe that it is in their interests.

Secret swaps

Spy swaps have occurred all over the world, although most of the locations for such exchanges remain a secret. During the Cold War, however, the divided German city of Berlin was the scene of many spy trades between East and West. These included the 1964 exchange of Soviet spy Konon Molody for Greville Wynne (1919–1990), a British spy imprisoned in a Soviet labour camp.

▶ The Glienicke Bridge, a crossing point between the American sector of West Berlin and East German territory during the Cold War. It hosted many spy swaps and is known as the 'Bridge of Spies'.

◀ In 1960, CIA pilot Gary Powers (1929–1977) was flying over the Soviet Union photographing Soviet missile sites when his Lockheed U2 spy plane was shot down. The announcement by the Soviets of his capture raised tensions between the sides during the Cold War. Powers was found guilty of espionage and sentenced to ten years' imprisonment.

▶ Soviet spymaster Rudolph Abel (see page 32) was imprisoned in the United States in 1957 but was exchanged for Gary Powers. The two men walked slowly past each other over the Glienicke Bridge during their 1962 exchange.

▲ An exchange between the two superpowers takes place on Glienicke Bridge, Berlin. In February 1986, four communist agents were exchanged for the Soviet dissident Anatoly Shcharansky (1948–) and four western spies.

Spy swapper extraordinaire

Wolfgang Vogel (1925–) was an East German lawyer who acted as a paid middleman and arranged the swaps of more than 150 spies between the superpowers and their allies during the Cold War. Vogel was involved in the swap of Abel and Powers (below, left) and he also secured the 1981 swap of East German agent Gunter Guillaume (see page 30) for eight West German, British and US agents.

▼ Another famous divide between East and West in Berlin was Checkpoint Charlie, the scene of a military stand-off in 1961 between US and Soviet tanks and troops. A museum devoted to the Cold War now stands nearby.

Trading information

In certain circumstances, secret services from different nations work together and share top secret information. For example, after the 11 September attacks on the USA in 2001, the CIA and the Russian SVR are believed to have shared some intelligence in order to fight terrorist threats. Similar collaborations occur between rival secret services in the battles against computer crime and global drugs trafficking.

Silicon spies

Spies and the services they work for have changed greatly since the end of the Cold War. Enemies and targets have altered, cooperation with other security forces has increased and in many countries, secret services have become more accountable to their people. Some of the greatest changes have come with the increased use of new technology.

▲ This is a Predator UAV (unmanned aerial vehicle), which has been used to carry out low-level surveillance missions during the wars in Afghanistan and Iraq. In 2002, one of these flying robots, equipped with Hellfire missiles, performed a successful assassination attack on a vehicle carrying a senior al-Qaeda terrorist in Yemen.

Spying without spies

Today, machines perform vast amounts of spying. Satellites intercept and relay communications signals, computers analyze email and internet traffic while unmanned robotic drone aircraft and even small unmanned submarines scour the skies and the seas collecting visual and communications surveillance. The fastest growing area of spying in the last 20 years has been computer-based. Large computer networks can be hacked and broken into, their files stolen and the contents decoded to discover important secrets. Individual computers can be fitted secretly with a keystroke recorder, a small device which records thousands of key presses and replays them at a later date to reveal a user's passwords and what they were typing. Spying software can take screenshots and transmit them secretly to another computer for analysis. With so much information now kept digitally, computer sabotage, such as the release of a computer virus onto a computer network or the erasing of a machine's hard disk drive, is a very real threat.

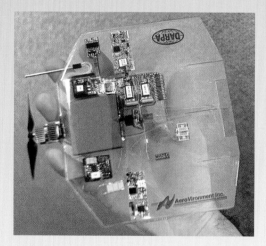

▲ This Black Widow MAV (micro aerial vehicle) has a wingspan of just 15cm and weighs less than 60g, but it can carry small video and still cameras. Similar MAVs are expected to enter service in the near future, spying secretly in places too restricted or dangerous for human agents to operate in.

Electronic monitoring

Every single day, billions of messages are sent around the world as phone or fax calls, emails, texts, radio signals or satellite transmissions. The secret services of many countries have found high-tech ways of intercepting and monitoring some of these communications to try to uncover important intelligence. Sophisticated filtering and tracking software scans millions of messages, seeking out those that contain certain keywords that may interest a secret service. The largest electronic monitoring system of all is Project Echelon, a system so top secret that some of the nations believed to be involved, including the USA and UK, have yet to admit publicly it exists.

Changing threats

During the Cold War, many nations were aligned with one of the two superpowers, the USA or the Soviet Union. In the 21st century CE, the boundaries between friend and foe are becoming more blurred. Conflicts and threats to security come from many sources, including nations or groups suspected of owning WMDs (weapons of mass destruction) such as nuclear weapons. In the past, secret services often concentrated on building large spy networks in a small number of rival countries. Today, secret services act globally, and frequently their targets are not rival secret services but terrorist groups such as al-Qaeda, and major crime syndicates. It is difficult for security services to infiltrate these groups, so other types of spying, including electronic surveillance, have to be used.

▲ In 1998, a terrorist attack resulted in a massive bomb blast close to the US embassy in Nairobi, the capital of Kenya. The blast killed 70 people and left more than 1,000 injured.

▼ The communications radomes of Menwith Hill in north Yorkshire, England, are believed to be the largest electronic monitoring station in the world, and may be part of Project Echelon. Although on British soil, the facility is run by America's NSA.

Biometrics

Establishing the identity of people who work in protected areas and have access to sensitive information is vital in industry, government and the military. Spies have tricked security systems over the centuries by donning disguises and using stolen or false ID, but the arrival of biometrics systems makes this deception tougher.

▼ The iris is the coloured band around the black pupil of an eye. It has around 400 distinct features, many of which can be measured by an iris recognition system. Images of the iris are taken by a video camera, and the system's software then compares the features to those it holds in its memory to work out whether the person is allowed or denied access. Iris scanning systems often take several rapid images of the eye to ensure that the pupil is moving. This protects against intruders trying to pass off a colour image of an eye as the real thing.

Biometrics systems dispense with smartcards, passwords and ID cards which could be lost, stolen or forgotten. Instead, they use sensors, computers and software to collect data about a person's unique physical features, such as their fingerprints, the size and scale of their facial features or their eyes. These systems then compare the data they have captured to the details they hold in their memory to check whether the person is who they are claiming to be. Biometrics systems are used to authenticate a person so that they can gain access to a protected area. When fitted to an electronic lock, they can allow or prevent access to rooms, computers and even vehicles.

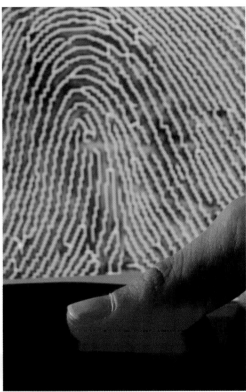

▲ A fingerprint scanner uses infrared light to capture the details of a fingerprint in 3D so it cannot be fooled by a high-quality paper copy of the correct print. Fingerprint scanners are being used as electronic locks on some security computer systems.

The future for spies

The digital age has changed spying forever. The vast majority of secret service staff now work from offices, using computers and other forms of new technology. But this does not mean human spies out in the field will disappear in the near future. While computers are expected to perform increasingly large amounts of intelligence work, the need for people to analyze, report on and make decisions based on this information will remain. Out in the field, human agents will always be required in certain crucial situations to perform difficult yet valuable work. For example, only experienced human spies have the ability to uncover key sources of top secret information, to turn and recruit agents from another country or develop a relationship with a new contact.

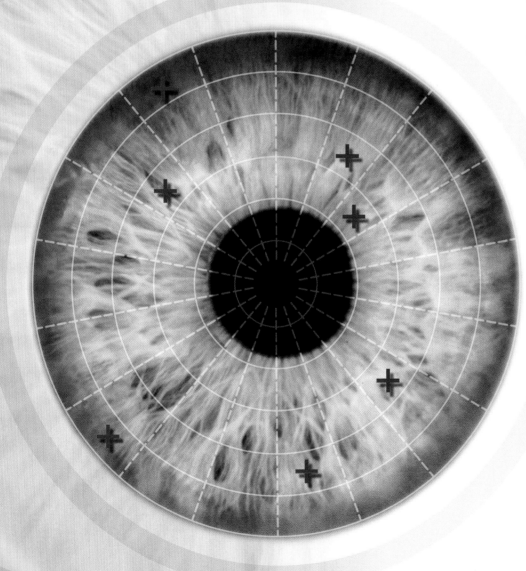

SUMMARY OF CHAPTER 3: TECHNIQUES AND EQUIPMENT

How are secret messages protected?

Spies use a range of ways to protect or disguise messages. They can be hidden in everyday objects. Messages can also be passed on to a courier, who ferries them to the intended receiver, or they can be sent over the airwaves using radio or another form of wireless communication. Many secret messages are protected by using a code, to make their contents unreadable unless the recipient knows the key.

Why are people and items disguised or concealed?

Concealing and disguising people and objects allows them to pass through areas without being detected. Hidden messages and weapons can pass through security checks, and concealed spy tools can prevent a spy being caught if their room, house or bags are searched. Spies often disguise themselves so that they blend in with their surroundings and do not attract attention.

Is spying performed without spies?

Yes, spy satellites are taking pictures and intercepting wireless communications all the time. Powerful computer systems search through emails and web pages while cameras, sensors and robotic surveillance machines keep watch over many places. Yet the need for human spies in some situations will remain.

A microscopic research camera is mounted on a bee's back

Go further...

 Try to solve the codes and cryptic puzzles at the NSA teaching website:
www.nsa.gov/programs/kids/standard/foyer/index.shtml

Take the interactive espionage quiz and learn more about spying techniques during the Cold War:
www.cnn.com/SPECIALS/cold.war/experience/spies/

Read about the skills and techniques that the FBI uses to tackle cases, and discover detailed reports of missions around the world:
www.fbi.gov/kids/6th12th/6th12th.htm

Hidden Secrets by David Owen (Firefly Books, 2002)

 Counter-terrorism analyst
Monitors and assesses the plans, leadership and capabilities of terrorist groups and their links to other groups or governments. Produces short, medium and long-term reports.

Signals intelligence officer
Telecommunications expert responsible for searching for new communications signals, identifying them and developing practical ways of collecting them.

Foreign language instructor
Trains secret service staff to speak foreign languages, and improve their knowledge of slang and new words.

 Visit Bletchley Park, the legendary home of Allied forces code-breaking during World War II, and view the many exhibits, including an Enigma code machine.
Bletchley Park
Wilton Avenue
Bletchley
Milton Keynes
MK3 6EB
Telephone: +44 (0) 1908 640404
www.bletchleypark.org.uk/

See a genuine U2 spy plane, an SR71 Blackbird and a section of the infamous Berlin Wall at the American Air Museum.
Imperial War Museum, Duxford
Cambridgeshire
CB2 4QR
Telephone: +44 (0) 1223 835000

Glossary

arms embargo
An agreement made between some nations to stop the transfer of arms into or away from an area.

assassin
An agent paid to plan and carry out the killing of a person considered a threat to national security in some way.

biometrics
In the field of security, the technology used to measure and analyze features of the human body, such as the eyes or hands, in order to identify a person.

bugs
Hidden devices, usually containing microphones and a transmitter, which can collect conversations and other sounds.

CCTV
Short for Closed Circuit Television, a system of security cameras which monitor buildings or public places.

cipher
A form of code in which each letter of the alphabet is represented by another letter, number or symbol in a system.

Cold War
The hostile relationship between the Soviet Union and the USA, which started shortly after World War II but never broke into world conflict.

counter-intelligence
Information gathered, and activities conducted, to protect against spying by other forces.

cover
A false name, story and background which disguises the real name, work and purpose of a spy in enemy territory.

cryptology
The science of analyzing and cracking codes and ciphers.

cut out
A person who allows two spies to exchange messages or documents without meeting.

dead drop
A secret location arranged in advance for the exchange of packages, messages or payments, where the people involved do not meet.

decoy
Something or someone used to distract the enemy's attention.

defector
A person who has left their own country's intelligence organizations and volunteers to pass information to another country.

denied area
A location, which can be a large region of a country, a town, a building or a room, that is out of bounds or impossible for spies physically to enter.

double agent
An agent who has come under the control of another intelligence service and is being used against his or her original masters.

espionage
The technical term for spying.

handler
A case officer responsible for the control and handling of a spy in a mission.

industrial espionage
Spying on businesses or organizations to learn what new products and plans they have.

infiltrate
To secretly enter an organization or group in order to spy on it.

intelligence
News and information important to a country or group's security.

jib
An inflatable dummy issued to CIA agents from the early 1980s onwards to replace an escaping agent inside a car.

live drop
A site where people meet and pass on or exchange messages, documents or other items such as cash or equipment. It can also mean the act of meeting.

microdot
A technique using photography to reduce a message or document from its normal size to less than 1mm across.

mole
An enemy agent who infiltrates a security service and usually works there, sending intelligence back to a rival intelligence agency.

network
A group of spies who may or may not know about each other and are organized by one spymaster. Also known as a spy ring.

one-time pad (OTP)
Sheets of paper or silk printed with random number ciphers to be used to encode and decode enciphered messages.

polygraph
The technical term for a lie detector, a machine which electronically measures nervous reflexes to a series of questions.

sabotage
The destruction or serious damage of a physical object, such as a building, train track or bridge. Digital espionage is the damage or destruction of a computer's software or the computer itself.

safehouse
A hotel room, rented flat or another building which is considered safe, free of bugs and unknown to other rival spies. It can be used as a base for a mission or a meeting.

SDI
Short for Strategic Defense Initiative, and also nicknamed 'Star Wars', this is the US-led project for a missile and space satellite defence system which could destroy and repel hostile missiles.

signal site
A place agreed in advance where one spy can leave a mark or signal to let others know of an instruction, event or change of plan during a mission.

spy ring
See *network*.

spymaster
The supervising agent in charge of a network or ring of spies.

Abbreviations of organizations

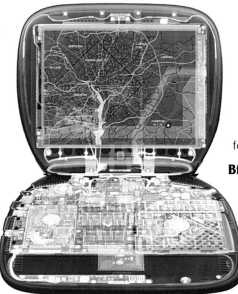

The term is also sometimes used for the head of a national intelligence or military intelligence service.

steganography
The science of hiding messages – concealing them in everyday objects or computer files for example, or creating microdots.

superpower
The term used to describe the USA and the Soviet Union during the Cold War era (1940s–1991) and since then, the USA.

surreptitious entry
The secret entry into a location through a break-in, lockpicking or disguise.

surveillance
The close observation of a place, person or group over time.

taps
Devices which allow the monitoring and recording of telephone calls.

ASIO
Australian Security and Intelligence Organization, founded in 1949.

BfV
German counter-intelligence agency, founded in West Germany in 1950.

BND
German foreign intelligence service, founded in West Germany in 1956.

CIA
The Central Intelligence Agency, founded in the USA in 1947.

DGSE
The French foreign intelligence service, founded in 1981, and the successor to the SDECE.

FBI
Federal Bureau of Investigation. National police force and counter-espionage agency of the USA, founded in 1908.

HVA
East German foreign intelligence service, formed in 1952 and worked closely with, or as a part of, the Stasi.

Interpol
Shortened name of the International Criminal Police Organization (ICPO) with over 170 member countries.

Interpol developed out of the International Police Commission, which was formed in 1923.

KGB
The former Soviet Union's key secret service, formed in 1954, and operational until the start of the 1990s.

MI5
The British security service, founded in 1909, responsible for UK counter-espionage activities.

MI6
The British secret intelligence service, founded in 1909, responsible for foreign intelligence.

Mossad
The shortened name in Hebrew for Israel's foreign intelligence agency, the Institute for Intelligence and Special Operations, formed in 1951.

NRO
National Reconnaissance Office, a US organization, founded in 1960, responsible for performing surveillance and collecting intelligence from satellites.

NSA
The US National Security Agency. was created in 1952, for collecting intelligence from communications.

OSS
Office of Strategic Services, a US organization, created in 1942, to perform spying and sabotage missions during World War II.

PLO
Palestine Liberation Organization, a political body representing the Palestinian people, founded in 1964.

SDECE
French foreign intelligence and counter-espionage agency which ran from the late 1940s until its replacement by the DGSE in 1981.

SOE
Special Operations Executive, a British World War II organization which specialized in working with resistance groups in Europe.

Stasi
The East German state security service, which operated from 1950 to 1989.

StB
The Czech intelligence and security service, formed in 1948.

SVR
Russia's foreign intelligence service which was founded in 1991 after the dissolution of the KGB.

Index

Acknowledgements

The publisher would like to thank the following for permission to reproduce their material. Every care has been taken to trace copyright holders. However, if there have been unintentional omissions or failure to trace copyright holders, we apologize and will, if informed, endeavour to make corrections in any future edition.

Key: *b* = bottom, *c* = centre, *l* = left, *r* = right, *t* = top

Pages: 2–3 Getty Images (Getty); 4–5 Getty; 7 Photos12; 8–9 Corbis; 10*tl* Werner Forman Archive (WFA); 10–11 Corbis; 11*t* Getty/Hulton; 12*tl* Mary Evans Picture Library (MEPL); 12*tc* Corbis; 12–13*b* Corbis; 13*tl* Corbis; 13*r* Corbis; 14*tl* DK Images (DK); 14*bl* Popperfoto; 15*tl* Corbis; 15*tr* Corbis; 15*b* Corbis; 16–17 Alamy; 16*bl* Public Record Office/National Archives, Kew (PRO); 16–17*c* Getty; 17*tr* Keith Melton/DK; 17*br* Getty; 18–19 Getty; 18*bl* Corbis; 18–19*c* Corbis; 19*b* Getty; 20–21 Corbis; 20*l* Corbis; 20*br* Corbis; 21*tr* Corbis; 22 Alamy; 23 Corbis; 24–25 Corbis; 24*l* Corbis; 24*br* Corbis; 25*tr* Corbis; 25*cr* Corbis; 25*br* Corbis; 26*c* Corbis; 27*c* Corbis; 28*l* Getty; 28*br* Corbis; 29 Deutsche Press Argentur; 30–31 Popperfoto; 30*tr* Getty/Hulton; 30*c* Associated Press (AP); 31*tr* Corbis; 31*cr* Popperfoto; 32*tr* AP; 32*bl* AP; 34 Corbis; 35 Corbis; 36 Corbis; 37 Photos12; 38*tl* Science Photo Library (SPL); 38*cl* Corbis; 38*bl* Getty; 38*tr* Corbis; 38*br* Getty; 39 Getty; 40*tr* Corbis; 40*br* SPI, California; 41 Corbis; 42*b* AP; 42*bl* AP; 43*t* Reuters; 43*br* Corbis; 44*tl* PRO; 44*crr* MEPL; 44*bl* Corbis; 44*br* Keith Melton/DK; 45 Corbis; 46–47 SPL; 46*bl* Corbis; 47*tl* DK; 47*b* Corbis; 48*cl* Corbis; 48*bl* Corbis; 49*cr* Corbis; 49*br* Corbis; 50*bl* AP; 51*tr* Reuters; 51*cl* DK; 52*bl* Keith Melton/DK; 52*l* Keith Melton/DK; 52*tr* Getty; 52*br* Keith Melton/DK; 54*bl* AP; 54*br* Corbis; 55*b* Corbis; 56–57*b* Reuters; 56*tr* Reuters; 56*c* AP; 57*t* Press Association; 58*bl* Corbis; 58*tr* SPL; 59 SPL; 60*bl* Corbis; 61*tl* Corbis; 61*b* Corbis; 62–63 Getty; 64 Corbis

The publisher would like to thank the following illustrators:
26–27*tc* Encompass Graphics; 33*c* Anthony Cutting; 50–51*c*, 53*t* Atlantean Picture Company

The publisher would like to thank the following people for their assistance with the photoshoot for pages 48–49:
Photographer: Andy Crawford
Model: Clive Gifford
Props purchased by Vicky Weber
Props donated by Giles Bywater, Carol Davis, Olly Denton, Clive Gifford and Kevin King